SPRINGING FROM THE PEWS

Mattar

ISBN: 978-1-913642-48-8

Book designed by Aaron Kent

Edited by Aaron Kent

Broken Sleep Books (2021), Talgarreg, Wales

Contents

springing from the pews   7
[ACT I]   8
[JOURNAL]   9
[ACT II]   10
springing from the pews   11
[ACT III]   12
[CONFESSION: METAL MAN]   13
[ACT IV]   14
[JOURNAL]   15
[ACT V]   16
[JOURNAL]   17
springing from the pews   18
[JOURNAL]   19
[ACT VI]   20
[CONFESSION: ITS OWN COMPANY]   21
springing from the pews   22
[JOURNAL]   23
[ACT VII]   24
[JOURNAL]   25
springing from the pews   26
[ACT VIII]   27
[CONFESSION: ITS FIRST STEPS]   28
[ACT VIII]   30

Acknowledgements   31

'Day Mattar's ground-breaking debut, exploring the experience of sexual abuse, marries form and content to stunning effect. This is a world of memory and reality where graceful lyricism co-exists with a brutal candour: a recurrent image of birds becomes the surprising and lovely 'murmuration of origami birds' - birds folded to evoke peace, the peace desired by the poetic voice who has 'for too long' carried his abuser's 'cock like a torch.'

The keynote of these shocking, moving, and sometimes wryly-funny poems is their fearless and genuinely challenging ambivalence; through the elegant device of parallel texts, Mattar's words enact the emotional bifurcation they express, of a desperate confusion on one hand and a taboo-defying celebration on the other.

Drawing on (among other things) the imagery of Catholicism, the questions Springing from the Pews asks - about innocence and confession, guilt and redemption - are unmistakably heartfelt: real, lived, questions. What, above all, does love mean, to a six-year-old child, or to the adults we become? Most urgently, perhaps, in the context of this poet's experience, what are the limits of acceptance, and what if transgression is not remembered as a simple matter of wrong?

These mature, accomplished poems, for all that they are troubled and troubling, remain triumphantly alive to the possibility of redemption, and to the redemptive power of the art they represent.'

- Alicia Stubbersfield

'A sensational, searing, and utterly singular achievement: what a first pamphlet to have written.'

- Andrew McMillan

Springing from the Pews

Day Mattar

springing

from the pews

cross the road   to a church

he was seventeen

the organ   sings

    i was six

the stained glass   hums

it happened
    in my bedroom

rain
    riots
on the concrete
my fists
        bounce
off the arched
wooden door

    but
it didn't hurt
    i wasn't
forced

storming the walls
the hems of my corduroys
soppy   slapping
my ankle

I want the priest to read verse
while I sob

i should hate him!

my little lamb pushing itself out
to candlelight
its white body   springing
from the pews

[ACT I]

[*spotlight*   *LAMB, centre-stage*   *shearing its own wool*]

VOICE TWO: [*left*] it was a
VOICE THREE: [*right*] a fantasy!
VOICE FOUR: [*behind*] he made-
VOICE FIVE: [*above*] he made it up!

LAMB: look
[*barks*] look!

this skin [*shorn wool, wilting*]
this skin [*blood shot eyes*]

[*table drops from the sky   chair drops from the sky   human body drops from the sky with pen*]

and you! [*rears*]
for nineteen years
carrying his cock like a torch.

VOICE ONE: was it rape?
VOICE SIX: it was rape!

[*above   a murmuration of origami birds   oscillates*]

sex clicks
into place along my spine, bends me over the sink.
brushing my teeth after a fuck, worried about the blood on the brush.
the tui and the bellbird's chorus, alien, through the window.
there's an alternate dimension where this didn't happen,
one where i stayed in New York, living above the little cupcake bakery,
a boy with turquoise hair
brings me turquoise roses.

maybe sex isn't dark there.
do i use a condom? am i as lucky? did i stop cutting? maybe
it's worse. twisted by ghb and crystal, limp
in a gimp sling, cold
sweat dripping from the ceiling. coming to
in a dark room. somewhere, i'm on PrEP.
can i afford it?

[ACT II]

[spotlight   centre stage, LAMB on interrogation stool]

CCTV CAMERA: *[groans into position]* your mum
is just on the other side of that door *[purrs]* there is nothing
to be afraid of

[...]

would you like some apple juice?

[distant rumbling]

can you tell us what happened?

[dry earth splits]

did he promise to give you something?

[a field of sunflowers ignites into screams]

did he say something bad might happen?

[a swan cracks the whip of her neck]

do you have anything else you'd like to tell us?

[the stage fractures and drifts]

*[LAMB drops a pebble into the audience   the audience ripples   the ripples grow
and grow]*

springing
from the pews

following cock
into the beach toilets
at pt. chevalier   jasmine
steaming on the fences

cold knees
on damp green tiles   jaw
locked in prayer
at the gloryhole

but
it wasn't cock i followed into my bedroom
it was love
but it wasn't love
it was rape
was it rape?

outside   two blackbirds hop
across blossom scattered pavement
another knocks back a worm
tilts its head

[ACT III]

LAMB: [*intimate*] you want to say no
shin split-open on the stairs running up after your six-year-old-self to say no.
no   trickling through leg hairs
soaking your sock. you want to say no with so much NO in your mouth
jaw clamped-open with NO but the word sort of fumbles
out and a spit bubble of no   pops
against the back of your six-year-old-head

[*darkness   rapid run of door slams*]

[CONFESSION: METAL MAN]

he palmed my small back
into a stoop

I'll be the robot
you be the nurse

we disappeared into the tent
my parts are broken

he lay down
untucked his shirt

can you fix me?
the skin around my mouth

creased
into two crescent moons

[ACT IV]

[*LAMB   ear pressed to a door*]

VOICE TWO: did it happen
the way you said it happened?

[*door battered to splinters*]

VOICE FOUR: but you wrote it down

[*a new door materialises*]

VOICE TWO: you read it out
VOICE FOUR: you coated the body bronze
VOICE TWO: you placed a blue buddleia in your six-year-old-mouth

[*the stage begins to tilt*]

you want to hear a voice   you hear your
LAMB: [*fists bleeding*] own slow breathing

i will love
anything that allows me to tilt,
fill the dish of their life, their day, their hour. let me express
love! i say to everyone, offering my whole body. take
my body! let me touch
the butterfly trapped under the silk
pulled over your hip bone

[ACT V]

CHORUS: WHAT WAS MISSING FROM YOUR LIFE THAT YOU'D MISTAKE RAPE
FOR LOVE
[*panicked wings*   *seizure of light*]

my flatmate holds her cat around the neck
and squeezes.

"if i could mistake his cock for love could he mistake my mouth
for a lover?"

she says he likes it, his handsome orange face ablaze in sun from the window,
white highlights under his half-closed eyes. his slow
breathing

"or a mother?
or a father?"

springing

from the pews

he has a little boy

karangahape road   churns
sat outside with a tea   I write

ten pages in my journal
use the word blistering
six times

commuters thud

he has a little boy

like coke bottles   lobbed
over the black paint-cracked railings
of the Mersey   yanked

he has a little boy

downstream
my headphones
tangle my pen
stutters out of ink
mid-

he has a little boy

sentence
the low sun   froths
behind a cloud   smears
a hot

he has a little boy

finger
across my cheek

he has a little boy
and a wife
i made a fake facebook account
just to look at them

give me back my life!
nearly bursts the living room   a harpoon in the wall
above where mum's fallen asleep in her dressing-gown

i want to say out-loud   HELP
i want to say next   YOURSELF

[ACT VI]

[*silhouette behind stained glass   illuminated*]

VOICE ONE: god help me god
help me poems will

[*flared nostrils pressed up against glass   steam, rising*]

never save us

[*cloven hooves kicking*]

maintaining abuse
keeping abuse alive
in these poems

[*window, shattered   leapt through*]

CHORUS: pull
ourselves together help
us help each other!

[*hysterical bell chime   louder   louder*]

[CONFESSION: ITS OWN COMPANY]

Front first on the wax paper. Face
through the hole in the massage table.
Eyes closed. Naked and bronze
as a suckling pig in the dim light.
I laughed when they got to my toes.
The warm oil made it easier to slip
between the gaps. Had to stop myself
from bucking. The three of us giggled.   Above
one either-side   like shaman
working to deliver from me
whatever there was to liberate.   Deep
strokes   neck
to shoulder   tricep
to forearm   hands
hips   then across   left
to right   taking over
where the other couldn't reach.
Arse-cheek slope   to hamstring. Dip
down   into calf   foot
then back around   and over in a loop.
I passed under their hands   like moving   water.
When I turned over with an erection
they said *that's perfectly normal*
and worked around it. I felt
so much of myself   rush
to that soft place   to make it hard
frantic   for one of them to   touch it
desperate   to escape
its own company. Lurching
like a body
pulling itself   from a grave.

springing

from the pews

amber eye of a gull
white scythe of its bill
fat orange bin bags   torn
apart   spilling

moon

i didn't tell them
that pleasing him

like a nipple
pressed against glass

came
naturally

rain

half a tomato
gaping

that somehow

ripped open
in the middle of the road

i felt special

[JOURNAL]

mum wants me to
STOP WRITING POEMS ABOUT ABUSE. says i'm
obsessed. that i hold it
too close. WHO ARE YOU? who am i
without it? hunched over a laptop, my whole body working against itself
in service of memory.

[ACT VII]

[*spotlight   pews, glowing*]

LAMB: [*genuflecting*] asking
can you take off your socks? can you take off
your pants   as if i knew

VOICE ONE: [*left*] did you know?

VOICE SIX: [*right*] that skin and risk
are a family that this was supposed to feel

VOICE ONE: like love?

[*a thurible weeps, centre stage   smoke submerges the audience*]

on a boat, cruising green water
fiord carved through mountains that step out,
push up against the Tasman sea, its finger pressed
into the arctic, between Aotearoa and Australia,
the warm Pacific. poetry won't make rape beautiful,
rape isn't a poem, it's a mountain.

face turned to the window, trying to understand.
all day fog has wreathed the peaks, hiding snow
and finally, like pulling cotton wool, the clouds part
and the mountains
steam.

springing

from the pews

we went downstairs straight after
and i coloured in a picture of a clown
holding up a flower
and gave it to him

[ACT VIII]

[*roof ripped open*]

VOICE ONE: in the name of the father and of the son and of the holy

LAMB: TRICK! [*on altar, gyrating*]

a-men [*close-up*] a-man that [*sharp*] look!
put his   [*sharper*] LOOK AT ME IN MY SIX-YEAR-OLD-FACE
PUT HIS   [*audience, hissing*] IN MY

VOICE ONE: [*frantic*] wouldn't you have done anything
to feel special   when you were small?
to double in height   feel powerful and loved
to blow out all the candles   eat all the cake

VOICE SIX: [*calm*] if we could go back   i wonder
how many would say we were pushed   [*pause*]
how many would say we jumped?

[*earthquake*]

LAMB: [*sinking into a crevice*] abuse
has made a mother of me
i've taken providence over it
[*reverb*] it is precious to me.

[CONFESSION: ITS FIRST STEPS]

School shorts loose around my knees
at the doctors. *He's been complaining about*

stickiness   haven't you? Mum explained
to the doctor. Older Indian woman

leaning against her desk. Lassos of skin
hooping her tired eyes. One hand resting in the other.

Pants down please. White latex gloves
snapped on. Her finger & thumb

like the curved side of two cold spoons   touching
my penis   pulling back the foreskin.

It was just another part of my body   something
to fiddle with   like my ear or my nose

     but
the sensation   of someone touching me there

clipped
a nerve.

If she'd looked directly at me
would she have noticed

                              the memory
she'd pinched   awake?

                    (bedroom
          uncle

                    door
          shut)

Could she have helped
as it staggered from me?   Wincing

taking its first steps
alone   in the sun.

It was me who would teach it to walk
to talk   to spell its own name.

[ACT VIII]

[LAMB, copper sunlight   audience, emerging from rubble]

LAMB: my six-year-old-skin wanted everything it touched to praise it
and everything that praised it   it touched

[blade   of wind]

take it [gestures] case it glass it frame it
have it studied   please [lowers face]
stop this from happening to

[LAMB   gripped by the neck   held out over the audience]

my skin is not a flag
do not raise me up in protest or pride
don't carry me to battles
don't wrap yourself up in me
don't make me dance on the roof when he dies

[the audience collapse into applause   LAMB dissolves into plea]

he was the love of my six-year-old-life he was
so handsome

Acknowledgements

Early versions of [EVIDENCE: ITS OWN COMPANY] and 'Springing from the Pews' have appeared, happily, in The Tangerine and The WoLF Poetry Anthology 2018.

The poems in this pamphlet made a home of me for ten years. I wrote the majority of them in Auckland, Aotearoa, and on train journeys back and forth from Liverpool to Manchester.

[EVIDENCE: METAL MAN] was my first attempt at writing candidly about abuse. I wrote its first draft in my second year at LJMU, under the tutelage of Alicia Stubbersfield. She encouraged me to rely on the strength of simple language to help bear 'the difficult stuff.' Alicia's loving direction and treatment of these poems has clicked on lamps and cleared fog. I'm so grateful to her.

Thank you Andrew McMillan, Carol Ann Duffy, and the bright brilliance of my peers at the Manchester Writing School, for helping wrangle the unruly herd!

Fiona Benson, Ilya Kaminsky, and Emily Berry, thank you for your poems, thank you for demonstrating how radical poetry can be in its truth telling.

My patient friends, Abi, Jon, Kim, Fiona, Steph, Steph, Helen, Amanda, Jess, Maria, Abbie, Dan, Brenda, who endure my ramble and keep me tethered to the earth. Love you.

I've asked my lovely family not to read these poems but the Sunday roasts, cups of tea in the garden, and sunset walks along the Mersey, were the perfect respite from writing them.

And Broken Sleep Books, Aaron! Thank you for working so hard to create this safe place. 'Pews' and I feel at home.

Spring free, Little Lamb.

LAY OUT YOUR UNREST